PARANORMAL
INVESTIGATIONS

# ESP, Superhuman Abilities,

## and Unexplained Powers

Alicia Z. Klepeis

Cavendish
Square

New York

Published in 2018 by Cavendish Square Publishing, LLC
243 5th Avenue, Suite 136, New York, NY 10016

Copyright © 2018 by Cavendish Square Publishing, LLC

First Edition

Website: cavendishsq.com

This publication represents the opinions and views of the author based on his or her personal experience, knowledge, and research. The information in this book serves as a general guide only. The author and publisher have used their best efforts in preparing this book and disclaim liability rising directly or indirectly from the use and application of this book.

CPSIA Compliance Information: Batch #CS17CSQ

All websites were available and accurate when this book was sent to press.

Library of Congress Cataloging-in-Publication Data

Names: Klepeis, Alicia Z.
Title: ESP, superhuman abilities, and unexplained powers / Alicia Z. Klepeis.
Description: New York : Cavendish Square Publishing, 2018. | Series: Paranormal investigations | Includes index.
Identifiers: ISBN 9781502628497 (library bound) | ISBN 9781502628503 (ebook)
Subjects: LCSH: Parapsychology--Juvenile literature.
Classification: BF1031. K55 2018 | DDC 133.8--dc23

Editorial Director: David McNamara
Editor: Kristen Susienka
Copy Editor: Rebecca Rohan
Associate Art Director: Amy Greenan
Designer: Joseph Macri
Production Coordinator: Karol Szymczuk
Photo Research: J8 Media

Printed in the United States of America

# Contents

Oracles, like the Oracle of Delphi pictured in this engraving, were thought to be able to speak to the gods.

# A Brief History of the Paranormal

Throughout human history, certain individuals have been believed to have powers beyond the normal realm. Sometimes, these powers fall into the physical category, like super strength. Other times, they are mental or spiritual powers. Regardless, for millennia, people have been captivated by those said to possess such superhuman abilities.

## From Ancient to Modern

Take, for instance, people with superhuman strength. A familiar yet ancient example is the Biblical story of a young boy named David. He is said to have defeated a giant warrior named Goliath. A normal boy would be highly unlikely to crush a much larger opponent in battle. However, to this day, many people use David as an example of superhuman strength.

There are also many modern examples. These include a mother lifting a car off her child or a person who can bend thick metal with her bare hands. Many modern fictional works celebrate such strength, too. Think about the human comic book character Bruce Banner, who turns into the Incredible Hulk, or Iceman, who can freeze objects or turn his body into ice.

From as far back as ancient times, many civilizations had traditions of people who could predict the future, contact the dead, or read peoples' minds. This tradition was especially strong in ancient Greece. Individuals would travel across the ancient world to visit the **oracle** at Delphi. Here, people consulted a priest or priestess, who would act as a medium, or in-between person, between humans and the gods. The priests and priestesses sometimes answered specific questions. Other times, they were asked to provide information about the future.

Delphi, however, was not the only oracle site. Olympia and Dodona were two other places where people consulted those with **paranormal** powers. Many ancient Greeks visited *manteis*, or seers, who lived in cities. Some of these seers even traveled with armies, using their powers to help military leaders make the right strategic decisions. The highly successful Alexander the Great was likely a believer in oracles. He visited the oracle of Ammon during the time of his military conquests. He had to travel hundreds of miles along the coast to Paraetonium (in modern-day Egypt) before heading inland to arrive at the oracle, located at the Siwah oasis in the Egyptian desert.

The treatment of people with paranormal powers has varied over time and from culture to culture. Many of ancient Greece's seers were well educated, highly paid, and respected by their countrymen. They were not on the fringes of society like many people with paranormal powers today.

At some points in history, those who claimed to predict future events were ridiculed and even ostracized by society at large. Psychics and other mediums were hunted as witches during the Middle Ages. Some were even burned at the stake, as during the seventeenth-century reign of England's Witchfinder General, Matthew Hopkins.

Matthew Hopkins claimed to hold the title of Witchfinder General.

## Modern Perceptions

Clearly the relationship between the general population and individuals with paranormal powers has fluctuated throughout history, and so has the strength in the belief in such powers. Today there remains interest—and belief—in paranormal powers and superhuman abilities. Many people have consulted psychics and mediums with the hope of learning about their future. Others are captivated by the idea that they might be able to send thoughts telepathically to others. Police departments sometimes engage the services of people claiming to have extrasensory perception (ESP) or other paranormal powers in order to solve crimes. And in different cultures, people continue to consult oracles.

It may seem strange that superhuman abilities exist outside the pages of a superhero comic book, yet there are people who claim they have X-ray vision, are able to scale tall buildings like a spider, or can balance a car on top of their head. Many find their accomplishments on the pages of newspapers or even in the *Guinness World Records* books.

Around the globe are both believers and skeptics in paranormal powers. People generally have pretty strong opinions on the matter. Some folks are absolutely convinced that ESP is a real phenomenon. Others think that ESP and superhuman abilities are nothing but a hoax. Scientists have been conducting research into both of these topics for many decades. They will likely continue to do so far into the future.

A brightly colored illustration of a fortuneteller adorns the doorway to a psychic's store.

# THE SCIENCE OF PARANORMAL INVESTIGATION

Humans have believed in paranormal powers for thousands of years. Yet it is only in the recent past that scholars have tried to use science to confirm—or deny—their presence. It may seem contradictory to use science to conduct paranormal investigations. After all, the word "paranormal" specifically refers to events or phenomena that are beyond the scope of normal scientific understanding.

In the late nineteenth and early twentieth centuries, a number of institutions were established to study paranormal phenomena. The Society for Psychical Research was founded in 1882 in Britain. Duke University in North Carolina had its Parapsychology Laboratory, established in the 1930s. In these and other institutions, scientists designed experiments and tests to determine whether individuals actually had the superhuman abilities attributed to them. Sometimes the results of these studies yielded positive findings. Other times subjects may have used trickery to fool the people conducting the tests.

To this day, scholars at prestigious universities continue to conduct paranormal investigations. They publish their findings in journals, books, and newspapers. Many people still believe that paranormal powers are real. They want to change the minds of the world's skeptics and naysayers. Who knows what the future of paranormal investigation will bring? Perhaps only those with **precognition** know the answer!

# NELLA
## A PSYCHIC EYE

*How to see into the mind, the future, and the world beyond*

JONES

with Mandy Bruce

In her book, Nella Jones discusses cases she has helped solve and how people can use the powers within them.

# The History of ESP

O n a Saturday night in April 1974, a famous painting called *The Guitar Player* was stolen from Kenwood House in London, England. A woman named Nella Jones heard about the crime. As she focused her mind on the painting's whereabouts, a map began to appear in her head. She sketched this map onto paper. She marked two crosses on her drawing.

Nella Jones shared her ideas with the police. As one might imagine, they were very skeptical. Nevertheless, the police took a chance. They headed to the location where Jones had told them the painting's frame could be found. Sure enough, they found the picture frame—just where she had told them to look. Then Jones described where the painting itself could be found: in a cemetery. Surprisingly, the painting was not damaged. The police—and many others—were shocked at how accurate Nella Jones's information had been. They even wondered if she'd been involved in the crime. Her name was cleared, however, when the real thieves were found.

How did Nella Jones know where the stolen painting was located? Where did her information come from? Her extensive knowledge of the painting's whereabouts did not come from using her five senses. She hadn't seen the painting at the time of the theft. She hadn't heard the footsteps of the robbers as they fled the crime scene. Nor had she touched, felt, or tasted the painting at that exact moment. Perhaps she got her info by extrasensory perception, or ESP. Nella Jones is just one of a number of people called psychic detectives. They are believed to use paranormal powers to help solve crimes.

## The Basics of ESP

Think about how you gather information each day. You might hear your teacher explaining math concepts during class (hearing). You might see a red traffic light and know to stop your bicycle (sight). You might know it's nearly dinnertime when the scent of vegetable soup wafts up to your bedroom (smell). You might feel your big toe at the end of your sneakers and know it's time for a new pair (touch). Or you might discover that the milk is too old when you take a sip (taste). People use their five senses to make meaning out of everyday events. This is called sensory perception. Many people around the globe believe that there is a "sixth sense." This is ESP.

Students are using their senses of sight and hearing to learn information from their teacher.

So what exactly is ESP? There are many different ways to explain it. Some say ESP is any perception that occurs outside of the five known sensory processes. Others describe ESP as the ability some people have to get information about the present, past, or future without using their five main senses. The term was first used in the late nineteenth century.

Hubert Wilkins (*right*) arrives in Antarctica. He conducted psychic experiments there while helping search for a crashed plane.

## Three Phenomena of ESP

Most resources describing ESP include three specific phenomena within its realm: **telepathy**, **clairvoyance**, and precognition. Telepathy is the transferring of thoughts between people. Sometimes people refer to telepathy as "mind-reading." This is a much-loved trait for characters in novels or popular TV shows like *Star Trek* to possess, but it has its roots in reality.

Some experts say that a crisis is often the trigger for telepathic communication. A mother might have a feeling that her child has been hurt or is in danger. Twins are also said to have telepathic powers. An interesting anecdote comes from 2009, when fifteen-year-old Gemma Houghton suddenly got the feeling something was wrong with her twin sister, Leanne.

She hurriedly looked about their home for her. Eventually, Gemma found Leanne unconscious in the bathtub. Leanne had had a seizure and had slipped under the water. Luckily, Gemma arrived on time and administered first aid, saving Leanne's life. Some scientists use the term "twin telepathy" and say events like this one are not uncommon.

Telepathic incidents often involve close family members, as opposed to friends or acquaintances, yet a fascinating example of acquaintances testing out telepathic communication dates back to 1937. It involves two men: an explorer named Sir Hubert Wilkins and a writer named Harold Sherman. They met in New York, just before Wilkins was about to head out on a search expedition for a plane that had crashed in the Arctic. The two men had a conversation about whether telepathy would work as a means of communication, such as between someone in the Arctic and someone outside of that icy region.

Wilkins and Sherman devised their own experiment. While Wilkins was in the Arctic and Sherman was in New York, they tried to communicate telepathically. Three nights each week between 11:30 p.m. and midnight (New York time), Wilkins attempted to send Sherman mental images or pictures of his day. During that same half-hour time period, Sherman wrote down whatever thoughts came into his head. Sherman sent a copy of his thoughts to Dr. Gardner Murphy, a parapsychology researcher. Wilkins also wrote down his experiences to compare with Sherman's notes.

All together, the men did sixty-eight telepathic sessions, and the results of their experiment were fascinating. Sherman received many clear, powerful images from Wilkins's expedition. He described all kinds of specific events, from a house on fire to an Inuit funeral to Wilkins all dressed up for a fancy ball. Were any of Sherman's visions correct? Amazingly, a number of his impressions turned out to be accurate. Wilkins did attend an officers' ball and wore fancy clothes to the event. The house fire Sherman saw was actually an Inuit home that burned up. Also astounding, exactly on the day that Sherman noted, there was a funeral. While Sherman had thought the funeral was for an adult, it turned out to be for a child. So not every image he saw was exactly right, but the similarities between the two accounts were striking. The results of this telepathy experiment affected Harold Sherman so much that he spent the rest of his life dedicated to psychic research.

Skeptics might wonder whether Sherman and Wilkins could have cheated. It would have been very difficult. There wasn't much information about the expedition available until it had ended. Plus, other individuals were monitoring this telepathy experiment.

## Clairvoyance

Clairvoyance is sometimes described as "the ability to see remotely." To those not very familiar with ESP, telepathy and clairvoyance can seem very similar. While telepathy involves the linking of two individuals' minds, clairvoyance is the ability to visualize hidden or distant images. It's as if the clairvoyant person sees things through a psychic camera or telescope. Another term for clairvoyance is "remote viewing."

Perhaps it's easiest to understand clairvoyance by giving some examples. Let's say someone "sees" information about an event or an object without getting this information from another person's mind. According to Dr. Diane Hennacy Powell, people have used clairvoyance to find mineral deposits, hidden treasure, and even missing people. Some experts have also claimed that clairvoyance can be used to diagnose medical problems by seeing inside people.

Psychics use their minds to access their powers.

Edgar Cayce is one of the most well-known clairvoyants in history. Born in 1877, he suffered a brain injury at the age of three. After this traumatic event, Edgar Cayce began having psychic abilities. As an adult, Cayce gave thousands of clairvoyant readings to people. He was known as the "sleeping prophet" because he gave his readings to people while in an unconscious state. Cayce would put himself into this state. His technique was simple: he would lie on a couch, close his eyes, and fold his hands over his stomach. For many clients, Cayce would do readings just based on their names and addresses. The majority of people seeking Cayce's clairvoyant powers wanted information regarding their health. He was known to provide both medical diagnoses and treatment recommendations.

Edgar Cayce's fame grew tremendously in 1910. In that year, Cayce performed a reading for a homeopathic doctor named Wesley Ketchum. Dr. Ketchum thought he had appendicitis and was scheduled to have surgery. Cayce's reading showed a different health issue: a spinal condition that was putting pressure on a nerve. Cayce turned out to be correct. In October 1910, the *New York Times* wrote about Cayce in an article headlined "Illiterate Man Becomes a Doctor When Hypnotized." Throughout his life, Cayce was visited by many talented scientists and other important figures of the time, including Thomas Edison, Nikola Tesla, and Woodrow Wilson.

## PETER HURKOS, PSYCHIC DETECTIVE

Born in Holland in 1911, Peter Hurkos is one of history's best-known psychics. Like Cayce and a number of others, Hurkos seemed to get his psychic powers after a brain injury. In 1941, he fell off a ladder and was in a coma for three days. While in the hospital, he discovered he had new abilities, such as predicting future events.

Peter Hurkos gained fame for his work as a psychic detective. He often used psychometry to help solve crimes. Psychometry is the (supposed) ability to discover facts about a person or event by touching objects associated with them. For example, he might touch a piece of clothing belonging to a murder victim and then be able to "see" what had happened to him or her. According to Hurkos himself, "I see pictures in my mind like a television screen. When I touch something, I can then tell what I see."

Hurkos's abilities were tested at a research laboratory in Maine in the 1950s. Dr. Andrija Puharich was amazed to see Hurkos had 90 percent accuracy in the tests conducted. This outcome was much greater than that of any other person Puharich had ever investigated.

# Precognition

Precognition is when people can "see" events before they happen. Believers in ESP think this knowledge comes to individuals by extrasensory means. Even if they didn't use the word "precognition," humans have believed in this phenomenon since ancient times. People from ancient Babylon to Rome had certain techniques they thought would allow them to see into the future. Scrying, or using a crystal ball or other reflective surface, was one such technique. Sounds familiar, right? People seeking knowledge about their future today often seek out the services of a psychic, who very well may use a crystal ball.

Sometimes people with precognition get knowledge when they are dreaming. Ancient Egyptians believed in precognitive dreams that could predict the future or deliver a message from the gods. Information from dreams was used to make important decisions. This dreaming-the-future scenario persists in more modern times. Did you know some scholars say Abraham Lincoln predicted his own death by assassination? Just a few days before he was assassinated, President Lincoln is said to have told his wife and a few friends about a dream he had. In the dream, Lincoln walked into the East Room of the White House. There he saw a corpse covered in funeral vestments. The corpse was guarded by soldiers. When Lincoln asked who was dead, a soldier told him that it was the president—and that he had been assassinated. Sadly, if Lincoln did have precognition, it did not save his life. But this dream is typical in that most precognitive events are reportedly seen close to the time they will happen in reality.

People are also said to get precognitive information while awake. Often this information comes in the form of an intense image or vision. For example, a person might be about to board a plane and suddenly have a vision of a plane crash. Choosing not to board the airplane, he may find out later that it did indeed crash.

Stories of people who have experienced telepathic events, who are clairvoyant, or who see events in the future have been around for millennia. They are likely to fascinate believers and nonbelievers in ESP for many years to come.

## DEBUNKING MINA CRANDON

Mina Crandon

When most people think of Harry Houdini, the word "magic" comes to mind. However, the multitalented Houdini also became quite interested in exposing fake mediums and psychics. One of the most popular mediums of the 1920s was Mina Crandon, known as Margery, or the Blonde Witch of Lime Street. Mina was famous for conjuring the voice of her dead brother Walter.

During **séances** run by Mina in Boston, Houdini tried to debunk her abilities. At first, things seemed to be going in Mina's favor. Walter's spirit supposedly rang a bell box on command and tipped over a wooden screen. However, Houdini did not believe Walter's spirit was doing these things. Sure enough, Houdini felt Mina twisting and flexing in the dark room in an effort to get to the bell box (which lay under a table). He also felt her shift to tip the screen using her foot. When Mina was allegedly levitating a table using sheer mental force, Houdini reached out and found that Mina's head was actually lifting the table from underneath it. He published a pamphlet exposing Crandon as a fraud.

A group of people participates in a séance.

# CHAPTER TWO

# Investigating ESP

**P**eople have believed in psychic experiences since ancient times, but there seemed to be quite a surge in such beliefs during the nineteenth century in both the United States and Europe. In a movement called **Spiritualism**, many individuals claimed to have contacted the spirit world or possessed the ability to communicate with the dead. As this trend became more widespread, it started to include other paranormal phenomena like reading minds and even hypnotizing people. Even though a number of Spiritualists were proven to be frauds, interest in psychic experiences escalated. Some people wondered if there could be any scientific explanations for these varied experiences. Spiritualism certainly helped inspire the growth of the psychic research discipline, in part as a way to examine its followers' claims.

## The Society for Psychical Research

It is only in the recent past that people have started to investigate what we now call ESP through scientific means. An important development in the advancement of psychic research took place in 1882: a group of scientists and Spiritualists founded the Society for Psychical Research (SPR) in London,

England. One might wonder who is qualified to examine the sometimes "out there" claims that fall under the category of paranormal experiences. The SPR was made up of some of the brightest minds of its time. Among its early members were prominent physicists, philosophers, mathematicians, and even Arthur Balfour, who later became the prime minister of Britain!

The Society for Psychical Research was "the first organisation to conduct scholarly research into human experiences that challenge[d] contemporary scientific models." The SPR began putting psychic experiences into different categories, such as mind reading (or telepathy) and clairvoyance. It collected and investigated data from both the past and present. In addition to reading reports of individuals' spontaneous paranormal experiences, scientists also sat through séances. They learned how to identify fake mediums and to sort through what were tricks or illusions.

Of course, not all of the Society for Psychical Research's work was about exposing frauds. The SPR also worked extensively with people they believed to have real paranormal powers. Examples include a medium named Leonora Piper of Boston, Massachusetts, and Winifred Coombe Tennant in London, England.

One of the most important products created by the SPR was the two-volume study *Phantasms of the Living*. Published in 1886, this landmark in psychical research looked at and analyzed more than seven hundred personal experiences of visions and apparitions. Many were referred to as "crisis apparitions" where people see "life-threatening situations in another location."

To this day, this Society for Psychical Research continues with its mission. It conducts surveys about paranormal experiences and offers lectures related to telepathy, clairvoyance, and other psychic phenomena. The SPR also continues to publish its journal. Its archives are located in London and Cambridge, and scholars around the world take advantage of these tremendous resources.

# J.B. Rhine and the Parapsychology Laboratory at Duke University

In the 1930s, the center of paranormal research largely shifted from Europe to the United States. During this time, the Society for Psychical Research changed its focus somewhat from being more of an investigative organization to an educational one. Dr. Joseph B. Rhine was an essential figure in this next stage of paranormal research. Some sources say that a British explorer named Sir Richard Burton came up with the term "extrasensory perception (or ESP)" back in 1870, but Dr. Rhine really popularized the term, using it to include phenomena such as telepathy and clairvoyance. He also was instrumental in designing and conducting scientific experiments to test ESP at Duke University's Parapsychology Laboratory.

One of Dr. Rhine's most important experiments tried to prove the existence of telepathy. Initially, Rhine used regular playing cards. He would ask the participant to guess what playing card he was holding (without them being able to see it, of course). He discovered that many could. Rhine found that people tended to guess certain cards more often than others since they were familiar with the cards in a normal deck. So he decided to try something new. Rhine worked with psychologist Karl Zener to design a brand new deck of cards with totally different symbols. These "ESP cards"—now known as Zener cards—have the following five symbols:

Dr. J.B. Rhine

a star, a box, a circle, a cross, or wavy lines.

Rhine repeated his experiment using the Zener cards. He found that, once again, people were able to name the symbol on the cards without viewing them. Over time, Rhine tweaked this experiment. While initially he had participants separated by a screen from the person conducting the experiment, he later had them in separate rooms. Why did Rhine think that people were able to "read" the cards without seeing them? He believed that ESP "operated independently from the physical body."

Thanks in part to his 1934 book titled *Extra-Sensory Perception*, Rhine's ESP research became very well known around the world. Not everyone believed in the validity of Rhine's results, however. A number of scholars and scientists have criticized Rhine's consistently high results of ESP, stating that researchers have not been able to "replicate the phenomenon consistently across laboratories."

Rhine conducted research into ESP and paranormal phenomena until 1965, when he retired. He also established the Foundation for Research on the Nature of Man (now called the Rhine Research Center).

Around the globe, people still use Zener cards to test for ESP, and the Rhine Research Center continues to conduct ESP research. It also offers professional parapsychology courses online.

Both dice and Zener cards have been used to test for ESP since the 1930s.

# The Ganzfeld Procedure

Another popular method to test for telepathy or other forms of extrasensory perception is the **ganzfeld** procedure. Experimental psychologists started using this technique in the 1930s. It involves controlling the sensory input of the person being tested for ESP. The idea behind this sensory isolation is that subjects perform better on ESP tests when they are not distracted by sensory input (noises, sights, etc.). Why? Some say a person's subconscious mind can better receive psychic connections when it is not distracted.

One might wonder how researchers are able to isolate a subject's mind from his or her senses. In a standard ESP-ganzfeld test, the person being tested goes into a special soundproof room. He or she wears headphones that play **white noise**, which prevents the subject from hearing sounds. The subject also wears special eye coverings, sometimes made from ping-pong balls cut in half. This makes the visual field of the subject look white. The subject in this highly controlled environment is the receiver of information. In another room is a sender, who tries to send images, thoughts, or feelings to the receiver. The sender might be looking at a series of slides, a filmed sequence of events, or a randomly selected picture.

In an ESP-ganzfeld test, researchers focus on the receiver's ability to get information telepathically from the sender. During a thirty-minute procedure, the subject on the receiving end describes whatever feelings, thoughts, or images come to mind. This is called **free association**. His or her responses are recorded. Then the receiver is shown several different **stimuli**—the target one "sent" to him and three other ones. The subject is asked to

This man is participating in a ganzfeld experiment.

rank these stimuli based on how much they matched his thoughts, feelings, or images during the ganzfeld period. Researchers score a "hit" if the receiver gives the highest ranking to the actual target. For example, if the sender had "sent" an image of surfers on a beach during the ganzfeld period and the receiver ranked that highest of the four stimuli, it would be a "hit."

From a statistical point of view, the chance of the subject guessing the right stimuli is 1 out of 4, or about 25 percent. And yet, according to Cornell University researcher

Dr. Daryl J. Bem, there has been an average hit rate of about 35 percent across over forty-two studies conducted in ten different laboratories.

Criticisms of the ganzfeld procedure have included that receivers may have gotten the target information by using their "normal" senses. This could be the result of sensory leakage (subjects hearing sounds, glimpsing images, etc.) or by deliberate cheating. But scholars and believers in ESP continue

## CHARLES HONORTON

Charles Honorton was interested in how the mind worked from a young age. As a high-school student, Honorton corresponded with the world-renowned parapsychologist J.B. Rhine. He even spent some of his summer months at Rhine's Parapsychology Laboratory at Duke University and collaborated on "dream telepathy" experiments at the Maimonides Medical Center in New York.

Unlike some researchers, Honorton was not especially interested in working with gifted individuals. In a *Rolling Stone* article, he was quoted as saying, "I'm much more interested in developing techniques that will increase latent ESP abilities in unselected individuals."

Honorton founded the Psychophysical Research Laboratories (PRL) in Princeton, New Jersey, in 1979. Here he conducted a variety of experiments investigating psi phenomena (related to psychic faculties), ESP, and psychokinesis. Honorton published articles in a number of outlets, including the *Journal of Parapsychology* and the *Psychological Bulletin*.

to conduct ganzfeld tests and feel confident in their accuracy. Prestigious scholarly outlets like the *Journal of Parapsychology* and the *Psychological Bulletin* continue to publish work celebrating the accuracy and reliability of this test method as a way to "prove" that ESP exists.

# Vision-Impaired People and ESP

Some parapsychologists have hypothesized that blind (vision-impaired) people naturally develop psychic facilities superior to those of people with normal vision. Dr. Lance Storm of the University of Adelaide in Australia tested this idea with eighty-four subjects. Forty-two of them were vision-impaired, and forty-two were sighted people.

Before each session, a target picture was chosen from four pictures. The target picture was then put into an envelope. All four pictures were also put into another envelope. The experimenter did not know the contents of either envelope before the testing took place.

Each participant was presented with a target envelope during the trial. He or she then tried to describe the picture concealed in the envelope. The experimenter then removed all four pictures from the envelope (the target plus three so-called decoys). The experimenter described all four pictures to the subject. The subject ranked the pictures from one to four: one being the one that best corresponded to his or her previous descriptions and four the least similar to his description. Finally, the target picture was removed from its envelope. The experimenter could then score if the subject "hit" the target picture.

Contrary to the hypothesis behind this experiment, the sighted subjects performed better than the vision-impaired participants. The sighted subjects hit the target about 33.3 percent of the time, compared to 19 percent for the vision-impaired subjects. According to Dr. Storm's findings, the results might have been influenced by personality differences between the two groups. Overall, the confidence and enthusiasm of the sighted participants were higher than for the vision-impaired participants. But Dr. Storm ultimately said, "It cannot be concluded from the results of one experiment that sighted people generally have better developed ESP than vision-impaired people." He also suggested that future experiments would need to prioritize matching subjects in the two groups in terms of personality and attitudes.

## S. G. SOAL: MATHEMATICIAN AND FRAUD

Not all paranormal investigators conduct experiments with success or honesty. Sometimes, fraud occurs. S.G. Soal was a twentieth-century British psychic researcher and mathematician. A member of the Society for Psychical Research, Soal worked on several paranormal research experiments. For example, he performed more than 120,000 card-guessing trials as part of his telepathy research between 1936 and 1941. During this period, Soal did not find any significant evidence of ESP's existence.

Later in the 1940s, he conducted ESP experiments with a subject named Basil Shackleton. Contrary to his earlier work, Soal achieved highly significant outcomes in these tests. Other scholars in the field questioned Soal's results. Soal was reluctant to let other experimenters test Shackleton's abilities. After Soal's death, a statistician named Betty Markwick showed that Soal had "made changes to individual digits to create false hits." Soal also tampered with the findings in his work with another subject, Gloria Stewart. Creative math indeed!

In New York City, "Iceman" Wim Hof sits up to his neck in ice to set a world record.

# The History of Superhuman Abilities

O n a summer day in 2008, firefighter Chris Hickman and his crew were returning from a call when they saw a car that had flipped onto its side, the engine still running and the tires spinning, causing the car to be unstable. After shutting off the engine, the firefighters worked to stabilize the car. It was then that Hickman realized the driver's arm was trapped under the weight of the vehicle. Time was of the essence.

He quickly decided to lift the car himself. By his own estimates, Hickman thinks he lifted the vehicle a bit more than 1 foot (0.3 meters) off the ground. The Chevy Blazer weighed more than 4,400 pounds (2 metric tons)!

Feats of superhuman strength or abilities are fascinating. How can someone lift a car all by himself or scale a skyscraper with no ropes, or eat tons of metal (and live to tell the tale)? It's as if some people have superpowers like comic book heroes. Some scientists say that when people are faced with stressful situations, their bodies' bursts of adrenaline give them somewhat superhuman abilities. Others think people are always capable of such amazing feats but only do them in a crisis situation.

## URI GELLER: SPOON-BENDER EXTRAORDINAIRE

Uri Geller is one of the most well-known people claiming to have psychokinetic powers. A former Israeli soldier, Geller appeared before audiences around the world, where he is said to have changed the shape of fork tines, twisted house keys, and even bent silver spoons in half—just with the power of his mind.

When Geller appeared on *The Tonight Show* in 1973, his skills were put to the test. Instead of using his own props, host Johnny Carson gave Geller spoons and some other objects to use. Geller hesitated and seemed to struggle. Finally, he said that he didn't "feel strong." Some experts say that a person with paranormal powers may struggle to perform if they sense people are very skeptical of their abilities. Geller continued to dazzle other audiences with his PK talents right into the 2000s. Perhaps his *Tonight Show* performance was just an off night—or was it?

# Look Out for the Iceman!

People are often warned not to walk over thin ice to avoid falling into a body of cool water. The human body is not designed to get too cold. Normal body temperature is 98.6 degrees Fahrenheit (37 degrees Celsius). **Hypothermia** is a serious condition that occurs when someone has an abnormally low body temperature. It can result in death if not treated.

Wim Hof is an adventurer from the Netherlands. Nicknamed the "Iceman," he seems to have a superhuman ability to tolerate cold. In 2007, Hof spent seventy-two minutes outdoors at the North Pole wearing only shorts. He has run an Arctic marathon—shirtless—where the temperatures were −20°F (−29°C). And if those feats weren't impressive enough, the "Iceman" also is the world record holder for being immersed in ice (up to his neck) for an hour and fifty-two minutes. While the average person could not maintain a core temperature of 98.6°F (37°C) while immersed in ice, Hof can. He holds many world records for various feats involving the cold.

How does Hof survive such frigid temperatures without negative health effects? He claims to be able to control his heart rate, breathing, and even his blood circulation. Hof credits his superhuman abilities in part to a special practice called Tummo (meaning "inner fire"). This ancient meditation technique has been practiced by monks in Tibet for thousands of years. An explanation of how Tummo works comes from the Nangten Menlang Buddhist Medical Center:

> Using visualization, breath techniques and movement, we connect to our inner fire and generate it greater and greater. We work with our breath, bringing it to a higher level, and this changes our blood. This warm blood in turn affects our hormones. We … can experience the profound changes that result when we cultivate the Tummo fire and spread it throughout the body. This is not just visualization, but something real.

## Does Spiderman Really Exist?

The Petronas Towers in Kuala Lumpur, Malaysia, are among the world's tallest buildings. Standing 1,483 feet (452 m) high, these eighty-eight-story buildings make one dizzy just looking at them from ground level. Imagine climbing to the top of one of these colossal skyscrapers without ropes. Sounds impossible, right? Not if you're Alain Robert, sometimes referred to as "the human spider" or simply "Spiderman."

Alain Robert climbs a tall skyscraper near Paris, France, in March 2014.

Using only climbing shoes and his bare hands, Frenchman Alain Robert has scaled some of the world's tallest landmarks—from New York's Empire State Building to Paris's Eiffel Tower. Many of Robert's climbs are done illegally—after all, they are extremely dangerous, and a fall would be fatal. However, Robert loves the challenge. Sometimes he is even paid to scale tall buildings, like his 2003 ascent of the 567-foot (173 m) Bank of Abu Dhabi in Dubai, United Arab Emirates.

People around the world wonder how Robert is able to climb like this. Is he really a superhero? It does seem that Robert has some superhuman finger strength. He can do three pull-ups in a row with a single finger! His nimble, strong fingers seem to be able to find where to grasp window ledges or any other structural feature available. What's next for Alain Robert? It's likely to be a secret, but keep your eyes on the world's tallest buildings …

## Can You Eat That?

People around the world eat all kinds of things from insects to guinea pigs, but you'd be hard pressed to find someone who could eat the things Michel Lotito did during his life. Nicknamed Monsieur Mangetout ("Mr. Eat Everything"), Lotito ate about 9 tons (8.2 t) of metal in a period spanning about forty years. Say what?

When Lotito was still a boy, he had a disorder called **pica**. People suffering from this condition often eat items that are not food, like plastic or dirt. Around nine years old, Lotito started chowing on parts of his family's TV set. It's hard to imagine what possessed him to try eating dangerous things like glass or nails, but somehow, he survived—and kept eating weird things his whole life. In fact, he made a career out of it.

Mr. Mangetout digs into a metal meal at the 1997 London Motorshow.

When eating metal, Monsieur Mangetout first broke it up into small pieces. He also drank mineral oil to keep his throat moist. Among the non-food items Lotito ate during his life are beds, TV sets, bicycles, shopping carts, chandeliers, and even an airplane (which he ate between 1978 and 1980). You might be surprised to learn that Michel Lotito died of causes not related to his unusual diet.

Some sources say that Lotito had a super thick lining of his intestines and stomach and that's why he could eat the things he did. Perhaps the rest of us better stick to peanut butter and jelly!

## Humans or Bats?: Echolocation

Daniel Kish is a blind man living in southern California. He lost his sight when he was just one year old. But Kish developed what some might call a superhuman skill: **echolocation**. Some have even called him "a real-life Batman." He has been in the news for doing what many assume is impossible for blind people: riding a bike, climbing mountains, and even living on his own in the wilderness.

Most people associate the word "echolocation" with bats and dolphins. It refers to the process of locating faraway or invisible objects using sound waves that are reflected back to the sender from the objects. Kish makes clicking noises that shoot out into whatever environment he is in. The sound waves produced by the clicks bounce off objects, people, and other structures before returning to Kish's ears. This gives him a picture of what is around him.

Daniel Kish

Kish is not the only person who can echolocate. He is working to help others develop this skill. He runs workshops for vision-impaired people so they can also learn to "see" the world as well as he does. Kish believes that the brain is at least partly hardwired to echolocate but that people need to activate this ability. Not everyone agrees with him, though. Regardless, Kish is amazing in his ability to describe what he "sees" in tremendous detail.

## Psychokinesis: Mind Over Matter?

Rolling a pencil across a table without touching it. Bending a metal spoon using only one's mind. Getting a piece of furniture to lift into the air as if by magic. These are all examples of the paranormal power known as **psychokinesis** (or PK). Psychokinesis is the supposed ability to move objects using only mental effort.

For centuries, people have been intrigued by the idea of moving objects using mind power. When Spiritualism was at its most popular point—during the late 1800s—séances were all the rage. During these events, observers would claim to see objects move mysteriously, thanks to the power of psychic mediums. These objects were sometimes said to suddenly float or fly by people, apparently untouched by human hands.

Another example of a psychokinetic event is getting a clock to stop, usually in connection with some type of crisis. One such anecdote involves a man who was visiting his brother at the end of his terminal illness. The caretaking brother was wearing a watch, which his brother had given him as a gift. The ailing brother died at 7:25 a.m. A few minutes later, the caretaking brother looked at his watch. It had stopped at the exact moment of his brother's passing. Who or what caused the watch to stop? It could have been the dying brother as he faded out of existence, or it could have been the caretaking brother, shocked by the event unfolding before him.

A lesser-known form of psychokinesis is pyrokinesis. People claiming to have this ability say that they can control and extinguish a fire with only their minds. In some cases, they are even reported to be able to create a fire using only mental powers. This may seem to many like the stuff of urban legend. News stories from the last decade told of a young girl in Vietnam who set many things on fire with only her mind. But there are definitely differences of opinion regarding whether pyrokinesis exists. According to How Stuff Works writer Kate Kershner, "Our brains just can't generate enough energy to ignite any object." Stephen King created a pyrokinetic character in his 1980 novel *Firestarter*. Perhaps the mystery of whether pyrokinesis is real will continue to blaze on.

# NATASHA DEMKINA: THE GIRL WITH X-RAY EYES

In the early 2000s, a Russian teenager named Natasha Demkina claimed to have X-ray-like vision. She said her eyes allowed her to see inside other people's bodies. She also claimed she could make medical diagnoses about patients. Demkina attracted quite a following, including doctors, journalists, and patients who felt strongly that her powers were real.

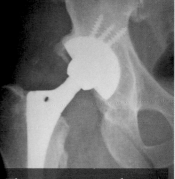

The X-ray image shows a person who has had a hip replacement.

As part of a Discovery Channel documentary about Demkina, she underwent testing of her X-ray abilities. One part of the test required her to "scan" six patients, all of whom had obvious medical conditions that appeared on (traditional) X-rays. These conditions included an artificial hip joint and a removed appendix, among others. The researchers told Demkina ahead of time what medical conditions she should be looking for. Natasha struggled with her readings, even failing to see the large metal plate in one man's head where a section of his skull was missing. Perhaps X-ray medical diagnoses are best left to the machines.

Some early psychokinesis experiments used dice to see if people could influence how they landed with just their minds.

# Investigating Superhuman Abilities

I n addition to capturing the imagination of everyday people around the world, superhuman abilities have caught the attention of scientists and other paranormal scholars. Scientific investigations of people with superhuman powers really began in earnest during the second half of the nineteenth century. While many people have strong beliefs in superhuman abilities, skeptics and naysayers have also abounded.

## Psychokinesis and Science

There have been many scientific experiments seeking to determine whether psychokinesis is real. Perhaps one of the most well-known took place at Duke University under Dr. J.B. Rhine, starting in the 1930s and 1940s. In the earliest version of this experiment, the subjects tried to use their minds to influence how dice fell from a cup. The experimenter told them to "wish" for a specific outcome (that is, for one particular side of the die to show up). Initially, the subjects threw the dice themselves. In later versions of Rhine's experiment, the dice were automatically thrown by a machine. Why? To avoid the possibility that the subjects might cheat or manipulate the dice.

In 1943, Dr. Rhine described the method and results of this experiment. Two dice were thrown by a machine for nine hundred separate trials. The subjects used their psychokinetic powers to try and influence which faces of the die came up. Remember that the odds of chance are one in six (or 16.67 percent) since each die has six different faces, or sides. Rhine reported that in his experiment, the "wished for" target faces came up 19.2 percent. Some might say this difference is pretty small, but to believers in psychokinesis, it may be significant enough to confirm their belief in such mental powers over the dice.

## The Air Force and Telekinesis

You might be surprised to find out that the US Air Force has also been interested in exploring psychokinesis. Astrophysicist Dr. Eric W. Davis wrote a 2004 research paper reviewing experiments testing telekinetic abilities. Why would the Air Force care about these paranormal phenomena? If people could control matter with their minds, this could be a tremendously powerful weapon in war. As Princeton University's Dr. Robert Jahn noted: "foreign adversaries could exploit … PK to induce US military fighter pilots to lose control of their aircraft and crash."

Dr. Davis's paper covered a variety of experiments, including the bending of spoons or forks with people's minds. He specifically mentions that Uri Geller made a spoon curve upward without using any physical force while talking at the US Capitol building. He also describes how aerospace engineer Jack Houck taught people at the Pentagon how to use psychokinesis to bend utensils using their minds. Davis's paper also suggests that PK has been successfully proven in scientific environments:

Scientifically controlled PK experiments at the Princeton University Engineering Anomalies Research Laboratory were conducted by Robert Jahn ... who reported that repeatedly consistent results in <u>mentally affecting</u> material substances has been demonstrated in the lab.

# Levitation

Throughout history there have been stories of people levitating themselves. These stories were often connected to religious experiences or miracles. For example, Christian tradition has a number of levitation examples. The seventeenth-century friar Saint Joseph of Cupertino was said to levitate on numerous occasions. Theresa of Avila, a sixteenth-century saint, supposedly became airborne when praying intensely.

Believers in human levitation say that people can learn the skill over years of practice. They think levitation is related to a person being enlightened. Can people really become so enlightened that they can float in the air? At this point in time, the scientific world says no. But a number of religious traditions (including Buddhism and Hinduism) might disagree.

This illustration depicts Saint Joseph of Cupertino levitating.

Despite these historical anecdotes, most people today would probably deny that people can levitate themselves or other objects just by using their minds. After all, when observed by scientists, many early psychics and mediums who levitated things during séances were proven hoaxes in the nineteenth and early twentieth centuries. Modern-day levitations typically fall under the realm of magical illusions, as performed by magicians such as David Copperfield and David Blaine.

## Echolocation in Humans

Scientists know all about how animals like bats use echolocation. But humans "seeing" without using their eyes seems a rather supernatural phenomenon, at least to some. Modern-day scholars have come up with a number of questions involving humans and echolocation. Can all people echolocate, or is it just a skill that vision-impaired individuals can develop? How does the process work?

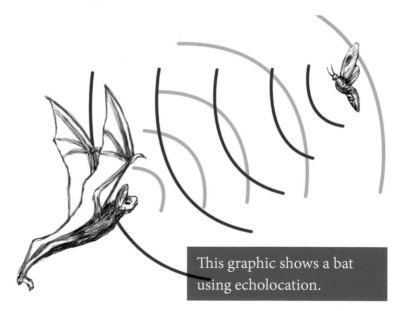

This graphic shows a bat using echolocation.

According to a 2013 article on the *Smithsonian* website, "the ability [to echolocate] isn't innate, but a number of experiments show that some people, at least, can teach themselves to echolocate." A few years ago, several research groups and labs began investigating humans' ability to echolocate. The basic principles of echolocation are the same for people as for other creatures. In short, a person must start by making a noise (like the high-pitched clicking sound a bat uses for this task). Most human echolocators, such as Daniel Kish, make a clicking sound by snapping their tongue tip against the roof of their mouth then pulling their tongue away. This may be a case of practice makes perfect. If a person can make a sharper click, it makes echolocation easier.

Humans can't make the roughly two hundred clicks per second that bats do when echolocating. However, even making a click every few seconds allows a person to continually update his or her "picture" of his or her surroundings.

A 2011 study at the University of Western Ontario in Canada found that echolocating might be easier for people who cannot see. They studied people trying to echolocate for the first time, using fMRI (functional magnetic resonance imaging). This imaging looked at which areas of the brain were active during the echolocation process. The results showed that the brains of the visually-impaired echolocators made up for their lack of eyesight by putting more effort (processing capacity) into sound instead.

## Investigating the "Iceman"

Numerous scientists have examined "Iceman" Wim Hof to learn more about his seemingly superhuman abilities to tolerate extreme cold. Dr. Maria Hopman, a medical doctor and professor at Radboud University Medical Centre in the

Netherlands, examined Hof while he stood in a cylinder filled with 1,543 pounds (700 kilograms) of ice. Under these conditions, a person's body is under major stress. Without special training, he or she would likely die of hypothermia. Yet, Hof's body temperature stayed constantly at about 98.6°F (37°C). Why is this? Dr. Hopman believes it may be that Hof was able to influence his autonomic nervous system. This system regulates a person's breathing, heart rate, and blood circulation. Normally, the autonomous nervous system is not consciously directed by a person—that is, the body makes this system function without thought or effort on the part of the individual (as if on autopilot, so to speak). And yet it appears that Hof could use his meditation and breathing technique to channel what some call his "inner fire," and make the necessary hormones or proteins to enable him to cope with the stresses of extreme cold. After rigorous testing and examination, it appears that the "Iceman" is, in fact, very real.

Wim Hof meditates in the snow in the Netherlands.

# EXTREME FEAR AND SUPERHUMAN STRENGTH

One minute a person can lift only a certain amount of weight, and the next, when in a situation of crisis, he or she manages to lift a car off a trapped individual. This very thing happened to Tom Boyle Jr. one summer night. A bicyclist had been run over by a car and was pinned underneath it. Boyle didn't stop to think. He just lifted … and the car was off the rider enough that another man could pull him out. Boyle himself is mystified about how he did this. "There's no way I would lift that car right now," he said later.

Where does superhuman strength come from? Professor Vladimir Zatsiorsky says that the fear centers of the brain progressively take away any restraints on performance. In essence, the more scared someone is, the more strength they may be able to utilize. But there is a limit to how strong fear can make people. Some scientists think that the brain may be able to draw on greater power reserves because of analgesia (the inability to feel pain). Under intense pressure, like seeing a person trapped under a car, the body may not feel its muscles ache, allowing superhuman feats to happen.

Feats of superhuman strength are common in comic books.

# CHAPTER FIVE

# What Does It All Mean?

There are many reasons why people should care about ESP in the modern age, even if science cannot guarantee its existence 100 percent. However, as many brilliant minds have noted for centuries, science may not explain everything in this world. Writer D.F. Marks notes that "Investigation of paranormal claims has failed to find any repeatable paranormal phenomena, yet beliefs in such phenomena are extremely prevalent ... Magical thinking is as evident today as it ever has been."

## Aspects of ESP Today

In the modern age, where science has been relied upon by many to explain the seemingly unexplainable, parapsychologists continue to conduct tests to prove aspects of ESP and other superhuman abilities. One important aspect of ESP is precognition. Some people might think it would be impossible to conduct a scientific study of precognition, but they'd be wrong—at least according to scholarship conducted at Cornell University. As a 2010 article in the *Cornell Chronicle* said, "It took eight years and nine experiments with more than one thousand participants, but the results offer evidence that humans have some ability to anticipate the future." Dr. Daryl Bem, a professor of psychology emeritus, says he had always been intrigued by precognition because "it's the most magical … It most violates our notion of how the physical world works."

Bem feels that precognition is the most mind-boggling of the psychic phenomena because, in his opinion, even though telepathy might be hard to believe, it seems remotely

Dr. Daryl Bem of Cornell University is a parapsychologist who has written on a variety of related topics, including ganzfeld.

possible in the realm of science. After all, electromagnetic waves can travel over huge distances, so perhaps the electrical impulses behind human thoughts can too. However, Bem says precognition is different because in order to sense an event that hasn't happened yet requires information to travel backwards in time. This would mean that "our classical view of the physical world is wrong," according to Bem. Even though he feels precognition "has the biggest wow factor" of the ESP phenomena, he has personally never experienced anything outside of his normal senses.

## ESP AND HUMAN NATURE

Since the dawn of humanity, people have longed to make sense of the world and all its mysteries. It seems plausible that people's belief in ESP and superhuman abilities plays into our innate curiosity. The modern era we live in is marked by anxiety and economic difficulties for many of the world's people. Over the course of history, such times have seen a surge in the belief of paranormal phenomena such as ESP. Why? Many think this is spurred by peoples' desires to make sense in a world that can feel out of control.

According to a 2005 Gallup poll, about 75 percent of Americans "profess at least one paranormal belief ... The most popular is extrasensory perception (ESP), mentioned by 41 percent." It's interesting to note that the word "normal" is often used to describe something that is characteristic of the majority. If that is the case, people who believe in the paranormal are actually normal, rather than outliers.

Whether in books, movies, or the research laboratory, people around the world continue to be captivated by telepathy. The idea of communicating thoughts and ideas without using one's normal senses is appealing. Wouldn't you like to send a positive message to a friend or relative who is ill? It might be great to be able to read the thoughts of someone who is far away or does not want to talk because of an argument. The list of reasons that humans believe telepathy could be useful is probably endless.

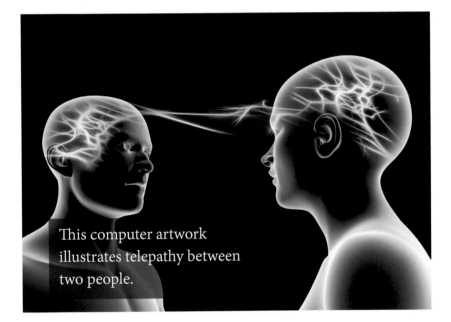

This computer artwork illustrates telepathy between two people.

A recent experiment involved a person in India saying "hello" and "ciao" to three other people in France. This may not sound very exciting until you consider that these greetings were communicated without a phone or email, just brain-to-brain communication. The research team behind this experiment involves scholars in Spain, France, and the United States. They are hoping to use telepathy to provide a means of communication for patients who may not have the ability

## MYSTERIES PERSIST

One topic that parapsychologists and neuroscientists
continue to investigate is the trance states that some
mediums use. Why? They want to know more about
how the mind works and its connection with the brain.
This mind-brain connection is a huge subject for future
research projects. So is twin telepathy. Researchers
are also still looking more deeply into psychography,
whereby a medium in a trancelike state supposedly
writes what a dead individual (spirit) guides them to do.

to talk. Alvaro Pascual-Leone, one of the study's co-authors,
acknowledges that this study was more about proving the
concept is possible. The ultimate goal is to "allow direct brain-
to-brain communication between people," a 2014 *Scientific
American* article states. Telepathy could be used in many
disciplines, from medicine to the military.

Like other ESP phenomena, people continue to believe in
and study clairvoyance. Many are fascinated—and perplexed—
by the idea that certain individuals can get information about
distant events and physical objects from outside of their five
senses. Some clairvoyance research in the 1990s surprised
many people. Yoichiro Sako was the founder of the ESPER
(Extrasensory Perception and Excitation Research) lab in Japan.
He discussed the results of one series of experiments involving
subjects being able "to 'see' letters and drawings on a target piece
of paper without the use of sight." Sako believes that children are
better at clairvoyance than adults.

Children sometimes demonstrate clairvoyant abilities.

The results of his lab's study of clairvoyance with children were shocking. There were many perfect hits among the thirty-five trials conducted. In the future, other institutions may choose to further investigate clairvoyance in children.

Perhaps Albert Einstein's views are most appropriate when speaking of the connection between ESP and science. He said, "The most beautiful thing we can experience is the mysterious. It is the source of all true art and science."

# NAYSAYERS

There is no doubt that throughout history, many people have doubted the existence of ESP and paranormal powers. For some of these naysayers, the root of their skepticism may be as simple as a "gut reaction"—that is, they just don't believe a human being can read someone else's mind or predict the future. Other naysayers might think all phenomena should be able to be explained by using our five senses. Scientists often tend to fall in the naysaying camp. Especially since the 1880s, scholars and scientists have tried to design experiments that could clearly prove whether psychic phenomena are real.

James Randi is one of the most famous naysayers in the ESP debate. Born in Canada in 1928, Randi was a magician and escape artist in his younger years before switching career paths to debunk those claiming to have ESP. Throughout his life, he has had a mission to expose people claiming to have paranormal powers. Randi was involved with debunking illusionist Uri Geller's powers on *The Tonight Show* back in 1973. He believes most cases of ESP are fake and has proven many such hoaxes himself. He was the subject of a 2014 documentary called *An Honest Liar*.

# GLOSSARY

**clairvoyance** The supposed ability to perceive things or events in the future or beyond normal sensory contact.

**echolocation** A process for locating distant or invisible objects by using sound waves reflected back to the sender from the objects.

**free association** A technique for investigating the unconscious mind, in which a subject reports all passing thoughts without reservation.

**ganzfeld** A technique used in parapsychology where sensory input is controlled, with the goal of improving results in telepathy tests.

**hypothermia** The reduction of one's body temperature to an abnormally low level.

**oracle** The place where a god is believed to speak through a person (such as a priestess in ancient Greece).

**paranormal** Referring to events or phenomena like clairvoyance that are beyond the scope of normal scientific understanding.

**pica** A craving or tendency to eat substances other than normal food (such as plaster, clay, or ashes).

**precognition**  Knowledge of an event before it happens, particularly of a paranormal kind.

**psychokinesis**  The supposed ability to move objects using only mental effort.

**séance**  A meeting where people try to make contact with the dead, especially through the efforts of a medium.

**Spiritualism**  A system of belief based on supposed communication with the spirits of the dead, particularly through mediums.

**stimulus** (plural: **stimuli**)  Something that acts to partly change the activity of the body.

**telepathy**  The supposed communication of ideas or thoughts by means besides the known senses.

**white noise**  A constant background noise, particularly one that drowns out other noises or sounds.

# FURTHER INFORMATION

Austin, Joanne P. *ESP, Psychokinesis, and Psychics*. New York: Chelsea House Publications, 2008.

Kallen, Stuart A. *ESP*. San Diego, CA: Referencepoint Press, 2012.

Nagle, Jeanne. *Investigating ESP and Other Parapsychological Phenomena*. New York: Rosen Education Service, 2016.

Owings, Lisa. *ESP*. Minnetonka, MN: Bellwether Media, 2014.

## Websites

**Ganzfeld: Hack Your Brain the Legal Way**
http://www.instructables.com/id/Ganzfeld-Hack-Your-Brain-the-Legal-Way
This website shows how to make a ganzfeld mask and gives some examples of sensory deprivation throughout history.

**How to Learn Telepathy**
http://www.metatech.org/wp/meta-abilities/learn-telepathy
This website explains what telepathy is. It also has a simple exercise you can try to see if you can send a message telepathically to another person.

**Mysteries and Science: ESP**
http://sd4kids.skepdic.com/esp.html
This website gives thorough but age-appropriate explanations of the various phenomena associated with ESP. It also shares some paranormal hoaxes through the ages.

## Videos

**CNN: Blind Man Uses His Ears to See**
http://www.cnn.com/2011/11/09/tech/innovation/daniel-kish-poptech-echolocation
This clip discusses Daniel Kish and his use of echolocation.

**The Guardian: French Spiderman**
https://www.theguardian.com/world/video/2015/apr/29/french-spiderman-scales-paris-tallest-building-video
This video shows Alain Robert, the French "Spiderman," scaling Paris's tallest building.

# BIBLIOGRAPHY

Begley, Sharon. "Why We Believe In ESP, Ghosts & Psychic Phenomena." *Newsweek*. 24 October 2008. http://www.newsweek.com/why-we-believe-esp-ghosts-psychic-phenomena-91915.

Bem, D.J. (1996). Ganzfeld phenomena. In G. Stein (Ed.), *Encyclopedia of the paranormal* (pp. 291-296). Buffalo, NY: Prometheus Books. Accessed September 30, 2016. http://dbem.ws/ganzfeld.html.

Bem, Daryl J., and Charles Honorton. "Does Psi Exist? Replicable Evidence for an Anomalous Process of Information Transfer." *Psychological Bulletin*. 1994, Vol. 115, No. 1, 4-18.

Bhattacharjee, Yudhijit. "Paranormal Circumstances: One Influential Scientists's Quixotic Mission to Prove ESP Exists." *Discover* magazine website. May 14, 2012. http://discovermagazine.com/2012/mar/09-paranormal-circumstances-scientist-mission-esp.

"Biography." Peter Hurkos website. http://peterhurkos.com/peter_biography.htm.

Bliss, Stasia. "NASA Confirms – Super Human Abilities Gained." Guardianlv.com. May 29, 2013. http://guardianlv.com/2013/05/nasa-confirms-super-human-abilities-gained.

"Brain-to-brain 'telepathic' communication achieved for first time." The *Telegraph*. September 5, 2014. http://www.telegraph.co.uk/news/worldnews/northamerica/usa/11077094/Brain-to-brain-telepathic-communication-achieved-for-first-time.html.

Carroll, Robert T. "ESP." Mysteries and Science website. June 6, 2013. http://sd4kids.skepdic.com/esp.html.

"ESP: What can science say?" Understanding Science website. http://undsci.berkeley.edu/article/esp.

"Extrasensory Perception: a brief history." The *Telegraph*. January 6, 2011. http://www.telegraph.co.uk/news/science/science-news/8244695/Extra-Sensory-Perception-a-brief-history.html.

Layton, Julia. "10 Real Events That Seem Like Hoaxes." How Stuff Works.com. http://history.howstuffworks.com/history-vs-myth/10-real-events-seem-hoaxes.htm.

Love, Robert. "Houdini's Greatest Trick: Debunking Medium Mina Crandon." *Mental Floss* website. October 31, 2013. http://mentalfloss.com/article/53424/houdinis-greatest-trick-debunking-medium-mina-crandon.

Melina, Remy. "7 Amazing Superhuman Feats." Live Science website. May 6, 2011. http://www.livescience.com/14048-amazing-superhuman-feats.html.

Soal, S. G., and F. Bateman. *Modern experiments in telepathy*. London, UK: Faber, 1954.

"William Eglinton Biography." Spirit Writings website. http://www.spiritwritings.com/williameglinton.html.

Wise, Jeff. "When Fear Makes Us Superhuman." *Scientific American*. December 28, 2009. https://www. scientificamerican.com/article/extreme-fear-superhuman.

# INDEX

# ABOUT THE AUTHOR

From ESP to jellybeans, **Alicia Z. Klepeis** loves to research fun and out-of-the-ordinary topics that make nonfiction exciting for readers. Klepeis began her career at the National Geographic Society. She is the author of numerous children's books, including *Bizarre Things We've Called Medicine, Goblins, Understanding Saudi Arabia Today*, and *The World's Strangest Foods*. Her middle grade historical novel *A Time for Change* was released in 2016. She has also written over one hundred articles in magazines such as *National Geographic Kids*. Klepeis is currently working on several projects involving unusual animals, American history, and circus science. She lives with her family in upstate New York.